SHADOW TO SACRED

A 90-Day Devotional Journey to
Repattern the Soul
through Truth, Tenderness, and Ritual
Volume I of the Holy Habits
Devotional Series

Angelyna Hawbecker

Sacred Ember Press

Published by Sacred Ember Press
ISBN: 979-8-9999040-0-3

For my children — Raised in the fire of my becoming. You were my first mirror, my fiercest love, and the reason I kept walking through the dark. This work is the light that found me on the other side.

To my deeply loved friends and those who walked beside me during this soulful journey, thank you. Your presence helped make this devotional a reality.

Special thanks to my family for embracing my growth, even when it was messy, and to the whispers of Spirit for continuously calling me home.

This devotional was born from the ashes of a life undone and the gentle embers of one reimagined. I am not a guru, nor do I get it right every day — I am a woman who was broken, remembered who I was, and began again. Each day in this book was lived before it was written. It's my prayer that these pages meet you where you are and offer a path forward, gently, fiercely, sacredly.

Angelyna

CONTENTS

INTRODUCTION

We begin in the dark — not because we are lost, but because that is where the truth waits to be reclaimed. This volume is not about fixing yourself. It is about remembering who you are underneath the masks, the habits, and the old survival scripts. It is about walking with your shadows — not to banish them, but to listen to what they've been trying to say.

Shadow to Sacred is a 90-day devotional invitation to teach your soul through honest reflection, sacred shifts, and daily rituals. This is a journey of remembering. Each week, we will explore a pattern that has protected us in the past but now keeps us small. Each day, we name it, offer it light, and choose a new way.

This is the beginning of your return — not to who you used to be, but to the sacred truth that was never lost. You carry both shadow and light — they are not enemies. They are torchbearers at either side of your path. Let the shadow teach you boundaries. Let the light remind you of your soul's shape.

You are not here to do more. You are here to see deeper.

You move with soul-tides, not clocks. You speak when the invitation aligns. You shine when you are seen — not because you need approval, but because your wisdom was always meant to be witnessed.

The world rushes. But you — you pulse.
In and out.
Quiet and true.
Sacredly timed.

WEEK 1: HIDING → VISIBILITY

Hiding once kept you safe, but now it keeps you small. Every day, there is a different reason we shrink…and also offers a path back to your truth, your voice, and your presence.

Hiding once kept you safe, it felt like the only way at the time. Many of us learned early that shrinking drew less attention, that silence invited less risk. Maybe you discovered that blending in meant fewer questions, fewer confrontations, fewer chances of rejection. For a time, hiding was survival — but as the years pass, it quietly robed you of life.

This week, you are invited to step gently into visibility. Visibility does not mean spotlight or performance. It does not demand you to be loud, impressive, or extroverted. True visibility is simply presence — the willingness to be here as you are, unmasked and unshrinking.

Every day will ask you to notice where you are still pulling back and to try one small act of stepping forward. As you do, you'll discover that your presence is not a danger, but a gift. When you allow yourself to be seen, you become a mirror of possibility for others.

May this week be a gentle unveiling, reminding you that you are safe to be seen and sacred in your becoming.

Day 1 – The Habit of Shrinking

The Old Pattern

You've learned how to shrink before you ever got a chance to shine. Somewhere along the way, being quiet became safer than being real.

You learned that your emotions were dangerous.

The Sacred Shift

You were not made to disappear. Your presence is not a threat; it's a blessing. When you show up fully, you become a mirror of what's possible for others.

The Ritual Replacement

Light a candle and whisper: "I take up space with grace."

Journal Prompt: Where do I still hide, and what am I afraid will happen if I am seen?

Bonus: Place your hand on your heart and speak your name aloud three times.

Day 2 – The Fear of Being Misunderstood

The Old Pattern

You tell yourself, "If I speak, they won't get it." So you keep quiet. You edit your light before it even hits the room.

You assume misunderstanding before connection can be born.

The Sacred Shift

You were not made to be universally understood—you were made to be truthfully expressed. The ones meant to hear you will feel you. You are not too much. You are connection that is waiting to be met.

The Ritual Replacement

Sit in silence and place your hand on your throat. Breathe deeply and whisper: "I allow myself to be seen and heard, even if not everyone understands."

Journal Prompt: What am I afraid will happen if I share my truth without apology?

Optional: Hum softly or speak a few lines of your truth aloud in a safe space—no editing.

Day 3 – The Mask of Competence

The Old Pattern

You've learned how to look composed even when you're falling apart inside. Perfection became your armor.

Overachieving became your disguise.

The Sacred Shift

You do not need to hold everything together to be worthy of love or belonging. Your softness is not a flaw—it is a holy invitation for others to breathe.

The Ritual Replacement

Sit with your journal and write down everything you're pretending to be okay with.

Whisper: "I am allowed to be seen in my becoming."

Let yourself cry if tears come. Let them soften the armor.

Day 4 – The Habit of Dimming

The Old Pattern

You sense when others shrink and instinctively dim your light to make them more comfortable.

You've confused compassion with contraction.

The Sacred Shift

You are not responsible for others' comfort around your brightness. When you shine, you permit others to do the same.

The Ritual Replacement

Light a bright candle in a dark room.

Stand tall and whisper: "I allow my light to rise."

Journal prompt: Where do I still dim my brilliance to stay small or safe?

Day 5 – The Fear of Rejection

The Old Pattern

Rejection taught you that silence is safer than risk. You learned not to ask for what you need.

You stopped expressing what you want.

The Sacred Shift

Your truth does not require agreement to be valid. Rejection is not a measure of your worth—it's redirection toward connection.

The Ritual Replacement

Write a letter to someone (you don't have to send it) expressing something you've been afraid to say.

Whisper: "My voice matters, even if it shakes."

Burn or bury the letter as a ritual of release.

Day 6 – When Silence
Becomes a Cage

The Old Pattern

What began as protection has become a prison. You've lost track of your voice. You're not even sure what your truth sounds like anymore.

You learned that speaking only brought pain.

The Sacred Shift

Your voice is still within you—quiet, maybe, but not gone. You are allowed to remember it. You are allowed to reclaim it.

The Ritual Replacement

Free write for 5 minutes: let your pen move without censoring.

Repeat: "I remember myself through my voice."

Let this be messy, unfiltered, and wild if needed.

Day 7 – Stepping Into
Sacred Visibility

The Old Pattern

You've held back, waiting for the right moment to be seen. But that moment keeps slipping away.

You fear being too much and not enough—at the same time.

The Sacred Shift

You are allowed to show up as you are—not perfect, not polished, just present. Visibility is not about performance; it's about presence.

The Ritual Replacement

Choose one way to be visible today: speak your truth, share your art, reach out, dress boldly—anything.

Whisper: "I am safe to be seen."

Journal Prompt: What did I feel in my body as I showed up?

MY NOTES

WEEK 2: PERFECTIONISM →
GRACE + PROCESS

"Have no fear of perfection—you'll never reach it." — Salvador Dalí.

Perfectionism whispers that if you could just get everything "right," you'd finally be safe. Safe from criticism. Safe from rejection. Safe from loss. Many of us learned to measure our worth in flawless performance — as if our humanness disqualified us from love. But perfection is a moving target, and chasing it is like running a race with no finish line.

This week invites you to step out of that endless chase and into the arms of grace. Grace is the reminder that you are already enough, even in the mess, even when the work is unfinished. The Divine doesn't ask for flawless offerings — only for your presence, your sincerity, your heart.

Each day will help you release a little more of the pressure to perform. You'll learn to embrace process, not perfection; progress, not polish. And in doing so, you may discover a freedom you didn't know you were missing.

May this week soften your striving, and may grace teach you the holiness of being human.

Day 1: The Habit of
Chasing Perfection

The Old Pattern

Perfectionism promised safety. If you could just get it all 'right,' no one would criticize, reject, or leave.

You learned to measure your worth in flawless performance.

The Sacred Shift

Perfection is a moving target. Grace is what remains when the target disappears. You are already worthy — even in the mess, even when it's unfinished.

The Ritual Replacement

Create a 'permission slip' to be human today.

Journal Prompt: Where do I feel the need to be perfect, and what does it cost me?

Bonus: Repeat aloud: "I choose grace over perfection."

Day 2 – The Myth of Getting It Right

The Old Pattern

You've chased "the right way" like it holds salvation. You pause before every decision, second-guess your instincts, and delay joy until certainty arrives. But perfectionism disguises itself as wisdom—when really, it's fear wearing a clever mask.

Finding safety in perfection only made it harder to achieve.

The Sacred Shift

There is no single right way. There's just your way. Learning, adapting, becoming. Mistakes are not failures—they're sacred experiments. You are allowed to try, to change, to begin again.

The Ritual Replacement

Choose one thing today to do imperfectly on purpose (messy hair, unpolished post, unscripted moment).

Journal Prompt: Where in my life do I delay action until I feel "ready" or "right"?

Whisper: "I free myself from the illusion of perfection. I walk in grace."

Day 3 – The Inner Critic's Grip

The Old Pattern

There's a voice inside that never seems satisfied. It picks apart your work, your words, your body. It masquerades as motivation, but it drains your joy and stunts your creativity.

You don't have to believe everything you think.

The Sacred Shift

That voice was born in protection, not truth. You don't need to silence it—you need to see it. Beneath every critique is a scared part of you asking for safety, not scolding.

The Ritual Replacement

Write down three recent self-critiques. Then respond to each with a voice of grace.

Journal Prompt: What does my inner critic fear will happen if I'm not perfect?

Affirm: "I meet my inner critic with compassion. I choose a kinder voice."

Day 4 – When the Bar Keeps Moving

The Old Pattern

Every time you get close to meeting your goal, the standard shifts. You raise the bar. You move the finish line. You deny yourself the sweetness of arrival.

Every step is meeting your goal. Even if it is a step back sometimes.

The Sacred Shift

You are allowed to celebrate. You are allowed to rest. Progress doesn't require punishment. Let yourself feel proud of where you are—even if you're not "there" yet.

The Ritual Replacement

Write a list of 5 things you've done this year that made you grow.

Journal Prompt: Why do I hesitate to celebrate myself? What would it feel like to let joy in now?

Whisper: "I honor the work I've done. I rest inside the process."

Day 5 – Unfinished Doesn't Mean Unworthy

The Old Pattern

You've equated completeness with worth. Half-finished projects. Unhealed wounds. Incomplete dreams. You shame yourself for what isn't "done" yet—as if unfinished means failed.

Toxic productivity doesn't make us worthy, it makes us burntout.

The Sacred Shift

The sacred lives in the becoming. Unfinished is not broken. You are still in process —and process is holy. Nothing in nature blooms all at once.

The Ritual Replacement

Sit with a project, idea, or part of yourself that feels incomplete. Breathe into it without judgment.

Journal Prompt: What beauty exists even in this unfinished space?

Say aloud: "I am a work in progress. I bless the process."

Day 6 – Letting Grace Lead

The Old Pattern

You've driven yourself with shame. With should-haves. With scarcity. You've believed that if you don't push, you'll fall behind.

Grace feels like a luxury you couldn't afford.

The Sacred Shift

Grace is not an escape; it's a guide. It doesn't mean avoidance. It means alignment. It means trusting that rest, softness, and presence are powerful enough to carry you.

The Ritual Replacement

Light a candle and repeat: "I allow grace to lead me."

Journal Prompt: What would change in my life if I let grace—not guilt—be the motivator?

Bonus: Do one thing slowly today, savoring the process without rush.

Day 7 – Progress Over Perfection

The Old Pattern

You've measured yourself by results. You've judged yourself in the middle. Perfectionism told you that unless it's flawless, it doesn't count. Anger has told you that it will never change.

Anger hidden as perfectionism only breeds more pressure to perform.

The Sacred Shift

Progress is sacred. Small steps matter. Forward is, even when wobbly. Your becoming isn't about flawless execution—it's about faithful return.

The Ritual Replacement

Choose one small act of progress and do it—no matter how tiny.

Journal Prompt: What progress am I proud of, even if it's not visible yet?

Affirm: "I honor the journey. I walk with grace, not pressure."

MY NOTES

WEEK 3: PEOPLE-PLEASING →
SOVEREIGN BOUNDARIES

"You were not born to disappear just to make others comfortable."
Boundaries are bridges—not walls. You are allowed to build them.

For many of us, safety once meant keeping everyone else comfortable. We learned to say yes when our souls screamed no, to bend and mold ourselves into what others wanted. Pleasing became a survival strategy — but over time, it cost us our authenticity. It kept us loved on the surface, but disconnected within.

This week calls you back into sovereignty. Boundaries are not walls that shut others out; they are bridges that allow true connection. When you honor your own needs, you are not selfish — you are truthful. Every time you choose authenticity over approval, you reclaim your power and your wholeness.

Over these days, you'll practice listening to your inner compass. You'll begin to notice where fear has kept you compliant, and how liberating it feels to speak your truth.

May this week help you remember that love does not require you to disappear — it asks you to be real.

Day 1 – The Habit of Pleasing

The Old Pattern

You've shaped yourself to meet others' expectations. You've said yes when your soul was screaming no.

Somewhere along the way, being liked became safer than being real.

The Sacred Shift

You do not have to be agreeable to be loved. Your truth is sacred. Your needs are not a burden—they are a compass. Every time you honor them, you come home to yourself.

The Ritual Replacement

Journal Prompt: Where have I recently said yes out of fear, not alignment? What did that cost me?

Practice: Say aloud to your reflection: "I choose authenticity over approval."

Day 2 – Approval Isn't Belonging

The Old Pattern

You've confused applause with connection. You've tried to keep the peace by keeping yourself small. You've equated being liked with being safe—but it's left you feeling unseen.

It's hard to belong anywhere, until you believe you already do.

The Sacred Shift

Approval is fickle. Belonging is sacred. True belonging doesn't require performance; it invites presence. The people meant for you won't need you to twist into someone else.

The Ritual Replacement

Journal Prompt: When have I traded truth for approval? How did that feel in my body?

Write: "I do not need to be understood by everyone to be valid."

Affirm: "I belong to myself first. That is where my peace begins."

Day 3 – The Disappearing Act

The Old Pattern

You tone yourself down. You speak more softly. You minimize your needs so others don't feel burdened. You disappear in the name of being "easy to love."

Love doesn't mean be less, perhaps it means to just be present.

The Sacred Shift

Shrinking is not love. Disappearing doesn't protect you—it erases you. You are worthy of taking up space—emotionally, spiritually, physically.

The Ritual Replacement

Stand tall and speak your full name aloud.

Journal Prompt: What part of myself do I tend to silence around others?

Bonus: Write a letter (to burn or keep) to someone you've shape-shifted for, reclaiming your truth.

Day 4 – Saying No Without Explaining

The Old Pattern

You feel like you owe everyone an explanation. You stretch yourself thin to avoid disappointing anyone. Guilt follows you every time you say no.

You learned you had to justify your decisions in order for them to be valid.

The Sacred Shift

"No" is a complete sentence. You are not here to justify your boundaries. You are here to live in integrity with your soul.

The Ritual Replacement

Write "No" in large letters on a page. Decorate it like sacred art.

Journal Prompt: What would it feel like to trust my "no" as holy?

Practice saying: "That doesn't work for me right now"— without adding anything else.

Day 5 – Boundaries Are
a Love Language

The Old Pattern

You worry that boundaries make you mean. You fear being misunderstood, pushing others away, or being seen as selfish.

Those who benefit from you not having boundaries, are those who get upset when you set them.

The Sacred Shift

Boundaries are not walls—they are bridges to honest connection. When you honor your "yes" and "no," you permit others to do the same.

The Ritual Replacement

Place your hand on your heart and whisper: "My boundaries are an act of love—for me and them."

Journal Prompt: Where have I abandoned myself to stay connected? What boundary would feel like kindness?

Day 6 – The Sacred Self-Honoring

The Old Pattern

You've mastered the art of making others feel seen, but rarely ask the same in return. You're always available, even when your soul is starving.

Self Sacrafice isn't the same as service, true service is giving from the overflow of your life, not an abandonment of it.

The Sacred Shift

You cannot pour from an empty vessel. Your needs matter. Your rest matters. You matter.

The Ritual Replacement

Create a "Do Not Disturb" ritual—even 20 minutes just for you.

Journal Prompt: If I stopped over-giving, what might come alive in me?

Place a small token (stone, leaf, charm) where you rest—a reminder that you are sacred.

Day 7 – Sovereign Heart, Sovereign Voice

The Old Pattern

You've feared that if you fully expressed your truth, others would walk away. So you've edited yourself—tone, truth, body, brilliance.

You have believed that you are too harsh or too loud or too _____ to be loved.

The Sacred Shift

Your authenticity is not a liability; it's your liberation. The ones meant for you will never need you to shrink.

The Ritual Replacement

Light a candle and say aloud: "I speak my truth with rooted grace."

Journal Prompt: What part of my voice is coming alive right now? Where is it asking to be heard?

MY NOTES

WEEK 4: CONTROL → TRUST + SURRENDER

"You do not have to hold the whole world together. That is the Divine's job. Yours is to breathe, to trust, and to allow what wants to become." — Unknown

Control often wears the disguise of responsibility. It tells us that if we don't hold everything together, it will all fall apart. For a time, it feels protective — a way of keeping chaos at bay. But in truth, control is a trauma response, born of fear, and it keeps us trapped in exhaustion.

This week, you are invited to loosen your grip. Surrender is not failure — it is freedom. Trust is not naivety — it is courage. To let go is to remember that the world is held by hands far greater than yours, and that you are safe to breathe, to rest, to allow what wants to become.

Each day will help you practice release. Little by little, you will discover that life does not collapse when you step back — it breathes more easily.

May this week give you the courage to trust what is becoming, even when you do not understand it yet.

Day 1 – Gripping the Reins

The Old Pattern

You've believed that if you don't stay on top of everything, it'll all fall apart. You micromanage your life, your healing, even your spiritual growth.

You decided that it would be better for you to just do it, since you would be blammed anyway.

The Sacred Shift

Control is a trauma response dressed up as responsibility. What if surrender isn't failure—but freedom? The Divine doesn't need your control, only your consent.

The Ritual Replacement

Hold something fragile (a leaf, feather, thread). Feel how delicate beauty lives outside your grasp.

Journal Prompt: What am I afraid will happen if I loosen control? What am I secretly hoping will happen if I do?

Whisper: "I trust what is becoming, even if I do not understand it yet."

Day 2 – The Illusion of Safety

The Old Pattern

You plan. You prepare. You protect every angle. The unknown feels unsafe, and surrender sounds like surrendering yourself to danger.

Surrender isn't always defeat, sometimes it's winning in disguise.

The Sacred Shift

Safety doesn't live in your plans—it lives in your presence. Trust is built not by perfect outcomes, but by real-time intimacy with your spirit.

The Ritual Replacement

Sit in stillness for 5 minutes without a plan. Just breathe.

Journal Prompt: What parts of me still believe safety only comes through control? Can I bless those parts with compassion?

Light a small candle and speak: "I am safe even in the mystery."

Day 3 – Surrender Isn't Passive

The Old Pattern

You've confused surrender with giving up. To let go felt like weakness, or like inviting chaos to win.

Giving up is a sacrifice that leaves you empty. Surrender is a strategy that makes you whole.

The Sacred Shift

True surrender is participation in the divine rhythm.
It's active trust. A holy agreement to show up fully without needing to know what comes next.

The Ritual Replacement

Write this mantra: "I show up. I surrender. I shine."

Journal Prompt: Where have I equated surrender with loss? What if it's a return?

Place one hand on your belly and one on your heart. Feel them rise together. You are enough without certainty.

Day 4 – Releasing the Outcome

The Old Pattern

You do everything "right" and still brace for disappointment. You track results, chase answers, and fear that if you don't get the outcome you want, it was all for nothing.

Trauma convinced you that by holding the world tightly, you might finally feel worthy.

The Sacred Shift

Your worth is not tied to outcomes. The beauty is in the becoming. You are here to live—not to control the ending of every chapter.

The Ritual Replacement

Tear a piece of paper into strips. On each strip, write one thing you're trying to control. Please place them in a bowl and breathe over them. Then burn or bury.

Journal Prompt: What outcome am I holding onto? Who would I be if I released it?

Affirm: "I do not have to earn arrival—I can be here now."

Day 5 – Sacred Surrender
Doesn't Mean Abandonment

The Old Pattern

When others let go, it meant neglect. When you let go,
it's followed by guilt. Surrender feels like giving up on people
—or yourself.

Abandoment whispers you must chase others, it asks you to
carry their peace as if it was yours.

The Sacred Shift

To surrender is not to abandon. It's to trust that your spirit
knows how to hold you—and that sometimes, letting go is the
act of love.

The Ritual Replacement

Write: "I can surrender without walking away from myself."

Journal Prompt: What does healthy surrender look like for me—
not forced, not afraid, but sacred?

Place a small stone or leaf on your altar: a symbol of surrender
that still holds form.

Day 6 – Let the Divine Lead

The Old Pattern

You've prayed… then took back the steering wheel. You ask for guidance—but feel uneasy waiting. You've been driving on empty, still afraid to pause.

Unworthiness still whispers in your ear," The Divine won't answer you until you are worthy"

The Sacred Shift

The Divine is already working on your behalf. Your job isn't to hustle—your job is to listen, align, and respond. The truth is that you are already worthy.

The Ritual Replacement

Light a candle and say: "I take my hands off the wheel."

Journal Prompt: If I believed that Spirit was already moving for my highest good, how would I live differently today?

Breathe in these words: "I am led."

Day 7 – Trusting the Becoming

The Old Pattern

You've been taught that transformation must be immediate. That trust should be earned instantly. You worry: Am I doing it right? Is it working?

You have been taught that results must appear instantly in order to be real.

The Sacred Shift

Becoming takes time. Roots grow quietly before blossoms appear. Trust is not a finish line—it's a rhythm you live into.

The Ritual Replacement

Plant a seed or water a plant today. Speak: "Even what is unseen is sacred."

Journal Prompt: Where am I growing, even if I don't yet see it?

Rest your hands over your heart and whisper: "I trust the slow blooming of my life."

MY NOTES

WEEK 5: SHAME → SACRED WORTHINESS

"Shame is the intensely painful feeling or experience of believing that we are flawed and therefore unworthy of love and belonging." – Brene Brown.

Shame whispers that you are broken, flawed, unworthy of belonging. It teaches you to hide, to apologize, to shrink. Many of us carry shame like an inheritance, passed down in words, in silence, in looks that told us we were "too much" or "not enough."

But shame is a lie. Worthiness is your birthright. You were not born broken, and you do not need to earn your holiness. This week, you will begin to return the story of shame to the fire.

Every day will help you peel away the layers shame wrapped around your soul. In their place, you will find the truth: you are sacred, even in the places you thought disqualified you.

May this week remind you that you are worthy not because of what you've done, but because of who you are.

Day 1 – The Lie of Shame

The Old Pattern

Shame taught you to make yourself small, quiet, and
apologetic. It told you that your flaws disqualified you from love.
So, you carried your story like a wound you had to hide.

Shame says, "you are not good enough, look what you've done."

The Sacred Shift

You were never broken. You are a sacred becoming, not a
mistake. Shame is not a truth—it's a story inherited from fear.
Your soul was never ashamed of you. The truth is, you are more
than enough, you are not what happened to you.

The Ritual Replacement

Write the word "SHAME" on a piece of paper. Circle it.
Surround the circle with everything that made you believe.
Then write outside the circle: "I return this story to the fire."
Burn it (safely) or tear it into pieces.

Journal Prompt: Whose voice taught me shame? What voice is
waiting to teach me worthiness? Speak: "I am still holy, even
here."

Day 2 – You Are Not a Problem to Fix

The Old Pattern

You've been taught to self-improve endlessly, to fix what's "wrong" with you before you're allowed to feel good, safe, or seen. Shame led you to believe that healing meant earning worth.

You are not the one who broke you, and so you are not the one who has to fix you.

The Sacred Shift

You are not a project. You are a soul. Healing isn't about becoming lovable—it's about remembering that you already are. Your worth is not a reward—it's a birthright.

The Ritual Replacement

Find a photo of yourself as a child. Place it on your altar or beside your bed. Whisper to the photo: "You don't have to be fixed. You just have to be loved."

Journal Prompt: What would I never say to this younger me? Why have I said it to myself?

Affirmation: "I am not too much. I am not broken. I am becoming."

Day 3 – The Mirror Isn't the Enemy

The Old Pattern

You've looked in mirrors and only seen flaws. Shame taught you to scan for what's wrong before allowing what's beautiful. It's as if the reflection could never hold the real you.

Shame has been used as a tool to turn the mirror against you, convincing you its reflection is the truth.

The Sacred Shift

The mirror only reflects what is in front of it. But shame distorts the lens. When you gaze with grace, you begin to see not just a body, but a becoming. Worth is not found in perfection—it's remembered through presence.

The Ritual Replacement

Stand in front of a mirror. Look into your own eyes for 30 seconds.

Speak this aloud: "You do not need to earn your beauty. You are sacred in your being."

Journal Prompt: What parts of myself have I judged that hold power or tenderness?

Optional: Place a drop of essential oil (lavender, rose, or cinnamon) on your wrists and say: "I anoint myself in truth."

Day 4 – Worth Isn't Conditional

The Old Pattern

You learned that love had to be earned. That approval required performance. Shame whispered: "Be better, or you'll be abandoned."

Shame has asked too many conditions of you. Love however, has never required them.

The Sacred Shift

You were never meant to audition for love. True worth is not transactional—it's intrinsic. You don't have to hustle to be held.

The Ritual Replacement

Write a letter to your younger self, beginning with: "You never had to prove anything to be loved…"

Journal Prompt: What belief about love and worth do I need to rewrite?

Affirm: "My worth is not conditional. I am enough, just as I am."

Day 5 – Unlearning the Shame Spell

The Old Pattern

You repeat certain patterns—not because you're flawed—but because shame embedded itself in your nervous system like a curse.

Shame will always reinforce itself. However, it does not have the final say.

The Sacred Shift

Shame is a spell that can be broken. Through breath, truth, and sacred ritual, you rewrite the energy of your body to speak a new language: love.

The Ritual Replacement

Inhale for 4 counts, hold for 4, exhale for 6. Repeat 4x.

Journal Prompt: What does my body still believe about my worth? What is ready to be re-taught with gentleness?

Touch your chest and say: "You are no longer a prisoner. You are a temple."

Day 6 – Sacred is Your Name

The Old Pattern

You've been ashamed of your desires, your body, your grief, your truth. Like sacred things were only allowed behind closed doors.

If shame can get you to question your worth, it will always have a place to live.

The Sacred Shift

Everything true about you is holy. Your longing is divine. Your softness is strength. Your body is not a mistake—it is a miracle.

The Ritual Replacement

Write your full name at the top of a blank page. Underneath, write: "I bless this name with sacred worth."

Journal Prompt: What parts of me have I called shameful that Spirit calls sacred?

Light a candle and say aloud: "I remember who I am. I am holy."

Day 7 – You Are the Offering

The Old Pattern

You thought you had to bring something perfect to Spirit, that your brokenness disqualified you from being a vessel.

You were taught to believe that broken meant unusable.

The Sacred Shift

You are the altar. You are the flame. You are the sacred offering. Not despite your wounds—but because of how you've carried them with grace.

The Ritual Replacement

Sit in stillness and whisper: "I offer myself, exactly as I am."

Journal Prompt: What part of me needs to be received by Spirit today, without fixing or hiding?

Optional: Place your hands palms-up on your lap and imagine golden light pouring in.

MY NOTES

WEEK 6: NUMBING →
EMOTIONAL PRESENCE

"I am safe to feel. I am strong enough to stay present."

Numbing begins as mercy. When the pain is too great, the body learns how to shut down, to protect you from feeling too much. But over time, numbing silences not only pain — it silences joy, connection, even your sense of self.

This week invites you to return to presence. To feel is not weakness — it is life. Your emotions are not here to drown you, but to guide you back to yourself. Tears are sacred water. Anger is sacred fire. Joy is sacred sunlight.

Each day, you'll take one small step toward thawing what's been frozen. You'll discover that your body and heart are strong enough to hold what arises.

May this week restore you to the language of your own emotions, reminding you that you are safe to feel.

Day 1 – The Cost of Numbing

The Old Pattern

You've learned how to turn down the volume on your pain. It was a form of survival. But over time, you stopped feeling the joy, too. You lost the language of your own emotions.

Anger, joy, fear, and shame, have each carried pain. But within them also lies you freedom.

The Sacred Shift

Feeling deeply is not a weakness — it's a portal. Your emotions are not here to drown you. They are rivers guiding you back to yourself.

The Ritual Replacement

Sit quietly and ask yourself: What feeling am I avoiding?

Journal Prompt: What has numbing protected me from? What has it cost me?

Optional: Run cool water over your hands or feet and say: "I come back into my body with gentleness."

Day 2 – Emotions Are Energy

The Old Pattern

You've been told you're "too sensitive." That emotions are distractions. So you tried to silence them, organize them, or spiritualize them out of existence.

You have been taught that your very essence is the enemy.

The Sacred Shift

Emotion is energy in motion. Grief moves. Anger protects. Joy expands. When you listen instead of suppressing, emotions become allies—not threats.

The Ritual Replacement

Sit in stillness. Choose one emotion you've felt lately (even if uncomfortable).

Ask: "What do you need to say?" Listen without judgment.

Journal Prompt: What emotion do I feel safest expressing? What emotion have I silenced the most?

Bonus: Dance, shake, or stretch for 3 minutes — let energy move.

Day 3 – Let the Tears Teach You

The Old Pattern

You've held in tears for so long, afraid they'd make you weak or burdensome. You learned to apologize when you cried, to tuck your feelings into quiet corners.

You have built a wall so the truth in your tears would not disturb the comfort of others.

The Sacred Shift

Tears are sacred messengers. They water the soil of becoming. When you cry, you aren't breaking down — you're releasing what your body no longer wants to carry.

The Ritual Replacement

Light a candle. Invite your tears with compassion: "You are welcome here."

Journal Prompt: What memory or feeling have I been holding back that wants to move through tears?

Optional: Place a warm cloth over your heart or eyes, and whisper: "Even my tears are holy."

Day 4 – Your Body Keeps the Feelings

The Old Pattern

You've numbed by leaving your body—disassociating, distracting, disappearing. But the body remembers. The tension in your shoulders. The lump in your throat. The tight chest. It holds what you haven't said.

The reason so many live with stress-related injuries, illnesses etc, is because we forget; our body keeps the score.

The Sacred Shift

Your body is not the enemy—it is your oracle. Every ache, every pause, every flutter of the heart is a message. You don't have to decode it all at once. You only have to listen.

The Ritual Replacement

Lie down and place one hand on your heart, the other on your belly. Inhale slowly for 4, exhale for 6. Repeat 5x.

Journal Prompt: Where in my body do I carry unspoken emotions? What might they be saying?

Optional: Massage your shoulders, jaw, or feet as you whisper: "I come home to you. I come home to me."

Day 5 – Sacred Rage, Sacred Grief

The Old Pattern

You have been told to "calm down," to "stay positive." Anger became dangerous. Grief became weakness. So, you buried them both. But buried fire does not disappear—it smolders.

You were taught you were not strong enought to handle big emotions.

The Sacred Shift

Rage is a boundary. Grief is a love that had nowhere to go. Both are sacred. Both are honest. Both are holy parts of healing.

The Ritual Replacement

Journal Prompt: Where am I still angry? Where do I need to grieve? What am I afraid will happen if I feel it fully?

Optional: Beat a pillow, stomp your feet, scream into a towel—or write an unfiltered letter and burn it.

Say aloud: "My emotions are not dangerous. They are divine."

Day 6 – Emotional Permission

The Old Pattern

You have felt like you need permission to cry. To rest. To need. To feel. You wait for the "right moment," or someone else's approval, before honoring what is real inside you.

You were made to feel as if your feelings did not matter.

The Sacred Shift

You are the authority now. Your feelings are valid without permission. Your soul does not need to be policed. You are safe enough to feel.

The Ritual Replacement

Place your hands over your chest and whisper: "It's okay to feel this."

Journal Prompt: Where have I withheld emotional permission from myself? Who gave me the message that it wasn't safe?

Bonus: Begin your day with this affirmation: "I trust what I feel. My emotions are wise."

Day 7 – Returning to Emotional Presence

The Old Pattern

You've lived in fragments—parts of you forward, parts of you hiding. You coped the best you could, and that was brave. But now it's time to be present.

You don't have to be fully healed to be fully here.

The Sacred Shift

Presence is your new home. You don't need to be numb to be safe. You are safe enough to feel. To breathe. To be.

The Ritual Replacement

Sit outside or by an open window. Feel the air on your skin. Let yourself arrive.

Journal Prompt: What does emotional presence feel like in my body today?

Closing affirmation: "I am present. I am feeling. I am healing."

MY NOTES

WEEK 7: FEAR OF SUCCESS →
EMPOWERED BECOMING

"It is safe to grow. It is sacred to succeed." Sometimes we don't fear failure — we fear what happens when we rise, who we might lose, and what we'll have to maintain.

Sometimes it is not failure we fear, but success. Rising means visibility. Success means change. Growth means some will not come with us — and part of us worries we will lose love if we grow too bright. So we dim ourselves, shrink back, or sabotage just before the breakthrough.

This week, you are invited to rise without apology. Becoming is not betrayal — it is your birthright. You do not have to abandon your softness to succeed; you simply have to stop abandoning yourself.

Each day, you will practice standing in your power with gentleness. You will learn that your light does not steal from others — it illuminates the way.

May this week give you courage to trust your own becoming, and to welcome the success that is already seeking you.

Day 1 – Afraid to Rise

The Old Pattern

You've pulled back right before the breakthrough. You've dimmed your light to stay relatable. You've chosen smallness so others wouldn't feel uncomfortable.

You have learned the language of smallness, mistakng it for safety.

The Sacred Shift

You were not made to stay hidden. You were made to rise and radiate. You don't have to abandon your softness to be seen. You just have to stop abandoning yourself.

The Ritual Replacement

Journal Prompt: When have I self-sabotaged or played small in the past? Why?

Stand in front of a mirror and say: "I do not fear my own becoming."

Day 2 – Who Do You Think You Are?

The Old Pattern

Every time you dared to dream big, a voice whispered, "Who do you think you are?" So you made yourself smaller. More agreeable. More "realistic."

Trauma whispers: "Don't think too highly of yourself." Truth responds: "You have always been enough."

The Sacred Shift

You are a child of the Ancient One. You carry the lineage of magic, wisdom, survival, and soul. Who do you think you are? You are remembering who you've always been.

The Ritual Replacement

Journal Prompt: What dream have I talked myself out of? Whose voice was I really hearing?

Write a new identity statement: "I am someone who..." (succeeds, heals, leads, creates, etc.)

Whisper your name aloud and affirm: "I was never too much. I was always meant to rise."

Day 3 – Upper Limits and Old Stories

The Old Pattern

Every time things started going too well, you found a way to crash. Get sick. Pick a fight. Miss the opportunity.

It's not self-sabotage—it's an old protection strategy.

The Sacred Shift

Your nervous system is learning how to hold more joy, more visibility, more you. That's why it feels so unfamiliar. But you are safe to expand. You are safe to keep the good.

The Ritual Replacement

Journal Prompt: What does "too good" feel like in my body? What's the earliest memory I have of shrinking back after success?

Sit in silence for 2 minutes and say: "I am safe to receive. I am safe to rise."

Optional: Light a candle and speak your current "upper limit"— then blow it out with gratitude and release.

Day 4 – *It's Not Selfish to Shine*

The Old Pattern

You've believed that if you take up space, someone else will lose theirs. That if you succeed, someone will feel less than. You've confused humility with hiding.

You were taught there is no room for you. But at Love's table there is already a place set for you.

The Sacred Shift

Your light does not steal from others—it shows them what's possible. When you rise, you rise for all the versions of you that thought it wasn't allowed.

The Ritual Replacement

Journal Prompt: Where did I learn that shining is selfish?
How would I live differently if I believed my light was medicine?

Write a short blessing for the version of you that hid to stay safe. Read it aloud.

Affirmation: "When I shine, I invite others to rise with me."

Day 5 – Worthy of What's Next

The Old Pattern

You've stopped yourself from wanting more because you didn't feel ready. Or worthy. Or healed enough. You've lived in the waiting room of your own becoming.

They lied to you, they said you would be worthy when the time was right. The truth is you already are worthy.

The Sacred Shift

You don't have to earn worthiness. You were born with it. What's next isn't a reward—it's a natural unfolding of all that you are.

The Ritual Replacement

Journal Prompt: Where have I held back because I didn't think I was "there" yet? What would I do if I believed I was already enough?

Create a "Worthy Now" list: five things you're ready for—not someday, but today.

Say aloud: "I am worthy of becoming. I am ready for more."

Day 6 – Let Success Be Sacred

The Old Pattern

Success has felt like pressure. A burden. A performance. Like something you must constantly prove, defend, or maintain. You forgot that it could be holy.

Success was never meant to be a contest.

The Sacred Shift

Your success is sacred because it's yours. Not because it's perfect. Not because others approve. But because it came through your pain, your healing, your soul.

The Ritual Replacement

Journal Prompt: What would sacred success look like for me? Feel like in my body?

Light a candle or place your hand over your heart and say: "I sanctify my success."

Bonus: Create a small ritual to honor a recent win—no matter how small.

Day 7 – Empowered Becoming

The Old Pattern

You've feared what might happen if you fully became who you're meant to be. What you might lose. Who might not come with you. You feared your own expansion.

You learned to shrink, believing smallness was the only way to belong.

The Sacred Shift

Becoming is not betrayal—it's the soul's return. You're not abandoning anyone. You're inviting the real you to take the lead finally.

The Ritual Replacement

Journal Prompt: Who am I becoming—and what do I need to leave behind to become them fully?

Optional: Write your name on a piece of paper, draw a circle around it, and speak a new identity over it.

Say aloud: "I honor what I'm growing into. I welcome the version of me I've waited lifetimes to become."

MY NOTES

WEEK 8: OVER-GIVING → SACRED REST + RECIPROCITY

"You were not born to burn out. You were born to burn bright."
You've poured endlessly into others, giving your time, your energy,
your empathy—sometimes until there's nothing left.

Even the Divine receives.

You've been praised for being strong, dependable, the one who is "always there." Giving became the way you proved your love — until you forgot to include yourself in the circle of care. Over time, over-giving leaves you empty, burnt out, disconnected from your own needs.

This week invites you to reclaim balance. Rest is not selfish; it is sacred. Reciprocity is the rhythm of the Divine — giving and receiving, pouring and being filled.

Each day, you will practice honoring your limits and listening to your body. You will learn that true generosity flows not from depletion, but from overflow.

May this week remind you that you are not here to burn out. You are here to burn bright.

Day 1 – The Habit of Over-giving

The Old Pattern

You've been praised for being the strong one, the helper, the one who's "always there." Somewhere along the way, you started measuring your worth by how much you give—and forgot to include yourself in that circle of care.

You came to believe that holiness was measured by how much of yourself you could give away.

The Sacred Shift

Giving isn't holy if it costs your wholeness. True generosity flows from overflow—not depletion. You are not selfish for needing rest. You are sacred for reclaiming it.

The Ritual Replacement

Journal Promt: Where do I give past my limits? What am I afraid will happen if I stop?

Practice saying aloud: "I release the need to prove my love by sacrificing my soul."

Create a simple Yes/No body check-in today. Before each task, ask: Does this drain or sustain me?

Day 2 – Who Heals the Healer?

The Old Pattern

You've carried others for so long, you forgot what it feels like to be held. You've believed that needing care makes you weak, that resting is a luxury instead of a right.

You have learned that "sooner or later" never really comes.

The Sacred Shift

Even the healer needs healing. Even the giver must receive. You are allowed to ask. You are worthy of restoration, not just resilience.

The Ritual Replacement

When was the last time I truly received care? Why is it easier to give than receive?

Take 5 deep belly breaths while repeating, "I am safe to rest."

Reach out—ask for help, or accept support where it's offered, even if it's small.

Day 3 – The Burnout Badge

The Old Pattern

You've worn exhaustion like a badge of honor. You've equated busyness with value. Somewhere inside, you've believed that collapsing at the end of the day proves you were "enough."

Pouring endlessly into others is not true help. It is the slow road to burnout.

The Sacred Shift

Your worth is not in your output. You are not more lovable when you're tired. You are not more spiritual when you're drained. Rest is not retreat—it's repair.

The Ritual Replacement

What story have I attached to being busy? What do I believe rest says about me?

Cross out (literally or symbolically) a "to-do" that's been fueled by guilt, not truth.

Create a Rest Altar: one object, one scent, one texture that invites peace. Sit with it for 3 minutes.

Day 4 – You Don't Have to Earn Rest

The Old Pattern

You wait until everything is done, until everyone else is okay, until there's "nothing left" before you allow yourself to stop. Even then, you feel guilty.

The safety of rest was stolen from you, leaving you unsure if stillness could be trusted.

The Sacred Shift

Rest is not a reward for suffering. It's your birthright. You don't have to be empty to deserve replenishment. You can stop before you break.

The Ritual Replacement

What would it look like to give myself permission to rest before I reach my limit?

Whisper this softly to yourself: "I don't need to earn this. I am worthy now."

Choose one restorative act today—extra water, a nap, a stretch, or even just stepping outside for fresh air—and do it without apology.

Day 5 – Love Shouldn't Hurt

The Old Pattern

You've been told that love means sacrifice. That to be a "good" partner, friend, child, healer—you must give more, stretch farther, hold everything together no matter the cost.

Trauma left you believing that love always costs too much.

The Sacred Shift

Love rooted in depletion isn't sacred—it's survival. True love includes you. When love is real, it doesn't drain your soul—it holds it.

The Ritual Replacement

Where have I confused love with self-erasure? Where have I accepted exhaustion as proof of care?

Speak this aloud: "I choose love that includes me."

Draw or write a symbol of reciprocal love—a relationship or vision that feels mutual, nourishing, balanced. Keep it visible this week.

Day 6 – The Sacred Art of Saying No

The Old Pattern

You've said yes when you meant no. You've taken on too much to avoid disappointing others. You've feared that "no" would make you unlovable or unkind.

You were taught that "real love" meant never having boundaries.

The Sacred Shift

"No" is a holy boundary. It doesn't close your heart—it protects it. Every sacred "no" makes room for your sacred "yes."

The Ritual Replacement

What have I said yes to that is costing me peace? What would it feel like to say no with love?

Write 2 gentle, firm "no" statements you could use when needed.

Speak this aloud: "Saying no to others is saying yes to myself."

Day 7 – Sacred Rest + Reciprocity

The Old Pattern

You've lived in imbalance. Always pouring, never receiving. You've called it love, duty, service—but it's left you depleted and disconnected from yourself.

A life of balance gives the soul the rest it longs for.

The Sacred Shift

Reciprocity is your return to right relationship—with others, with Spirit, with yourself. This is not selfishness. This is sacred remembering.

The Ritual Replacement

Where in my life is reciprocity missing? Where could I offer or receive with more balance?

Create a Circle of Return: draw a simple circle on paper and write inside it three ways you'll give—and three ways you'll allow yourself to receive.

Say aloud: "I give and receive in harmony. I rest in sacred balance."

MY NOTES

WEEK 9: COMPARISON → INNER TRUTH + UNIQUE LIGHT

"Don't dim your soul trying to match someone else's shine."
Comparison robs your spirit of its voice and your path of its beauty

Comparison is a thief. It robs you of joy, convinces you that you are behind, unworthy, or lacking. It turns others into measuring sticks instead of companions. And yet — your soul was never meant to match another's path.

This week, you are invited to return to your own truth. Your journey is not late, your light is not dim, your becoming is not wrong. The Divine does not deal in timelines or rankings; it deals in uniqueness, in presence, in authenticity.

Each day, you'll practice turning away from comparison and toward your inner compass.

May this week help you honor the light that is yours alone to carry.

Day 1 – The Mirror Is Not the Truth

The Old Pattern

You've looked outward to know if you're okay. You've measured your timeline, your body, your gifts, even your healing—against others.

Comparison cannot show you the true reflection of who you were meant to be.

The Sacred Shift

The mirror of others was never meant to define you. Your soul is not behind. Your journey is not off course. You are exactly where you need to be — You are becoming.

The Ritual Replacement

Journal Prompt: Where have I been comparing my path to others? What pain has it caused me?

Close your eyes and imagine a mirror turning into a window. Ask your soul: What do I see when I look through, not at? Affirm: "I walk the path that is mine. I honor the light that is only mine to carry."

Day 2 – The Lie of Not Enough

The Old Pattern

You scroll, watch, and listen—and somewhere inside, the whisper begins: "They're ahead. They're better. You're not enough." It doesn't matter how far you've come; the ache of lack sneaks in.

The thief will come quietly, draining your strength with the lie, "it won't matter why try?"

The Sacred Shift

Comparison is the thief of not only joy, but clarity. You were never meant to match their path. You were meant to reveal your own. Enough is not something you earn — it's the truth of your being.

The Ritual Replacement

Journal Prompt: When do I feel like I'm not enough? Who or what triggers this belief?

Practice a "soul inventory": list 3 things you've created, survived, or become in the last year. Name your own sacred becoming.

Affirm aloud: "I am not behind. I am blooming on time."

Day 3 – Sacred Incomparable

The Old Pattern

You've believed you need to be more like them — more
eloquent, more spiritual, more consistent, more perfect. You've
made someone else's life the rubric for your own.

Comparison whispers that you must be more like someone else,
but imitation only hides the beauty of who you are.

The Sacred Shift

You were never meant to be a duplicate. You are the only
version of you that will ever exist. Your way, your timing,
your voice — it's not a mistake. It's medicine.

The Ritual Replacement

Journal Prompt: Whose voice or path have I been chasing that
isn't mine? What parts of myself have I silenced to fit in?

Say this aloud: "I revoke the spell of sameness. I am
incomparable."

Draw or write one word or symbol that represents your soul's
distinct light. Keep it near you today as a quiet reminder.

Day 4 – You Are the Standard

The Old Pattern

You've waited for approval to trust your path. You've searched for someone who looks like you, speaks like you, lives like you— to permit you to be who you are.

Believing grace is for everyone but you denies grace the opportunity to show you who you are meant to be.

The Sacred Shift

You are the blueprint. You are the origin. You are the evidence that your way is valid. You are not meant to fit the mold — you're here to break it with grace.

The Ritual Replacement

Journal Prompt: Where have I been seeking permission instead of presence? Where have I looked for proof outside myself?

Practice: Write a "sacred declaration" beginning with: "I am the one who…"

Affirm: "I am the standard. My light is the proof."

Day 5 – From Looking Around
to Looking Within

The Old Pattern

You've looked outward to feel safe. You've assumed others must know better—more spiritual, more experienced, more "in tune." And in that pattern, your wisdom went quiet.

In silencing the voice within you, you have made room for the noise of others.

The Sacred Shift

Your truth doesn't get louder when others approve. It gets clearer when you listen. You were never meant to outsource your knowing. The voice you've been waiting for is your own.

The Ritual Replacement

Journal Prompt: What truths have I ignored because someone else told me otherwise?

Sit in stillness. Place your hand on your chest and ask: What is true for me right now?

Affirm: "I return to my inner knowing. I lead from within."

Day 6 – The Sacred Flame That Is You

The Old Pattern

You've felt like a flicker in a world full of flames—small, unseen, maybe even unnecessary. You've questioned if your light mattered when others seemed so much brighter.

The smallest flame can pierce the deepest dark. Your light needs no one else to make it shine.

The Sacred Shift

No one else has your flame. It may not roar—but it warms, guides, and ignites. The world doesn't need a louder fire. It needs your honest one.

The Ritual Replacement

Journal Prompt: What do I bring into the world that no one else can?

Candle ritual: Light a small candle and say: "This is my flame. No other can burn it." Sit with it in silence.

Affirm: "My light matters. It was never meant to be compared—it was meant to be lived."

Day 7 – I Belong to Myself

The Old Pattern

You've asked: Where do I belong? You've tried to earn a seat, match a vibe, mold your truth to fit the room. And still, something felt missing.

You have learned to find safety in conformity. But the gift has never been what you can do -- it has always been you.

The Sacred Shift

You don't belong by becoming someone else. You belong when you remember who you are. Home is not a place. It's the moment you stop trying to escape your essence.

The Ritual Replacement

Journal Prompt: When have I felt most like myself? Who was I when no one was watching?

Mirror ritual: Look into your own eyes and speak your name with reverence.

Affirm: "I belong to myself. My soul is my sanctuary."

MY NOTES

WEEK 10: DOUBT → DIVINE CONNECTION + FAITH

"Our doubts are traitors and make us lose the good we oft might win by fearing to attempt" – William Shakespeare.

Doubt often creeps in quietly — a fog that whispers you are alone, that the signs aren't real, that your prayers fall on silence. But doubt is not proof of absence; it is the place where faith is born.

This week invites you to meet your doubt with curiosity. To treat it not as a wall, but as a threshold. Faith is not the absence of questions; it is the courage to trust anyway. The Divine does not withdraw when you waver — it waits patiently for you to remember.

Each day, you will practice listening beneath the noise, finding again the quiet voice that has never left.

May this week restore your faith and remind you that you are always guided, even when you cannot see the way.

Day 1 – The Voice Beneath the Noise

The Old Pattern

Doubt sneaks in like fog — you don't always notice it at first.
It whispers that you're alone. That the signs aren't real. That
maybe this whole spiritual journey is just your imagination.

What if all that noise is really just a distraction to keep you from
seeing your own worth?

The Sacred Shift

Doubt is not your enemy. It's the place where belief is being born.
Faith is not the absence of questions—it's the courage to trust
anyway. The Divine doesn't disappear when you're
unsure. It waits patiently for you to remember.

The Ritual Replacement

Journal Prompt: When did I last feel doubt in my spiritual path?
What was I needing to feel safe or certain in that moment?

Practice: Sit in silence for 3 minutes. Breathe gently and place
your hand on your heart. Say softly: "I'm listening."

Day 2 – The Invisible Thread

The Old Pattern

You've asked for signs — then second-guessed them. You've questioned if your prayers went unheard. You've wondered if the silence meant abandonment.

They say the Teacher is always silent during the test. But the truth is, every test is silent -- and still, the Teacher remains.

The Sacred Shift

Connection isn't always loud. Sometimes it's a soft rhythm beneath the noise, an unseen thread weaving grace through your days. The Divine doesn't perform for your certainty. It abides with your soul.

The Ritual Replacement

Journal Prompt: What sign, sensation, or whisper have I dismissed as "just a coincidence"? What if it were real?

Practice: Recall a recent moment of peace, awe, or clarity. Revisit it in your body. Let it become evidence.

Affirm: "I am held by a sacred thread—even when I can't see it."

Day 3 – The Wisdom in Waiting

The Old Pattern

You've rushed to fill the silence. You've clung to outcomes. You've mistaken stillness for abandonment and delay for denial.

In the waiting, you are not abandoned. You are being invited to see the flowers blooming at your feet.

The Sacred Shift

Waiting is not punishment — it is preparation. Faith isn't forged in immediacy but in the places where clarity takes time. The Divine does not ghost you. Sometimes it pauses to let you grow into what you've asked for.

The Ritual Replacement

Journal Prompt: Where am I impatient for clarity or results? What fears sit beneath my hurry?

Candle ritual: Light a candle and sit with it for 5 minutes. Say: "Even in the waiting, I am not alone."

Affirm: "I am being guided, even when the way is not yet clear."

Day 4 – Silence Is Not Absence

The Old Pattern

You've heard nothing — and feared the worst. You've wondered if the quiet meant you were forgotten. Doubt has used silence as evidence against your worth, your gifts, even your belonging.

Silence is not rejection. It is the sacred pause that allows you to breathe.

The Sacred Shift

Silence is not abandonment—it's an invitation to trust. The Divine does not owe you noise. Sometimes the quiet is where the deepest truths are whispered. Sometimes it's where your soul is finally still enough to hear them.

The Ritual Replacement

Journal Prompt: When have I felt abandoned by Spirit? What stories do I tell myself when I can't "hear" guidance?

Practice: Sit outside or near a window. Close your eyes and listen—not for words, but for presence.

Affirm: "Silence is sacred. I am not alone in the quiet."

Mantra: "Silence is not absence. It is an invitation to trust."

Day 5 – Return to the Altar Within

The Old Pattern

You've searched outside yourself for certainty — books, mentors, rituals, rules. You've doubted your access to the Divine, believing you had to earn your place at the sacred table.

Altars are not built of stone and wood, but of heart and tears.

The Sacred Shift

You are the altar. Spirit lives in you, not outside of you. The deepest connection isn't something you chase—it's something you remember. You don't have to prove you're worthy to be met. You already are.

The Ritual Replacement

Journal Prompt: What spiritual rules or stories have made me feel "not ready" or "not worthy"?

Practice: Place both hands on your heart. Say aloud: "I return to the altar within." Sit for 5 minutes with eyes closed.

Affirm: "I am sacred space. Spirit meets me where I am."

Day 6 – The Leap That
Builds the Bridge

The Old Pattern

You've waited to feel ready. You've asked for guarantees before you moved. Doubt said, "Don't risk it unless, you're sure."

Having the path laid out before you does not make it stronger.

The Sacred Shift

Faith doesn't always feel solid at first. Sometimes it begins as a whisper and becomes a roar only after you leap. The bridge between fear and truth is built by your willingness to step.

The Ritual Replacement

Journal Prompt: Where am I waiting for certainty that may never come? What leap do I feel called toward — big or small?

Visualization: See yourself stepping onto a bridge made of light. Each step forward strengthens it.

Affirm: "As I leap, the path reveals itself beneath me."

Day 7 – I Trust What Lives in Me

The Old Pattern

You've handed your power to others—to gurus, systems, traditions and signs. You've questioned your inner voice so many times that it has gone quiet.

They say not every person who wanders is lost, perhaps the truth is, the path is made in the wandering.

The Sacred Shift

The deepest connection is not about following — it's about remembering. What you seek is already inside you. You are not a seeker lost in the woods. You are the flame that lights the way.

The Ritual Replacement

Journal Prompt: What wisdom inside me have I silenced or ignored? What might happen if I trusted it today?

Mirror ritual: Look into your eyes and say: "I trust what lives in me. I carry the spark."

Affirm: "I am the light I was waiting for."

MY NOTES

WEEK 11: IMPATIENCE →
SACRED TIMING

"What is for me will not pass me by."

The false clock ticks loudly, whispering you are late, behind, or running out of time. It presses urgency on your soul, convincing you that sacred work should happen quickly. But the soul does not bloom on demand — it blooms in season.

This week, you are invited to rest in trust. To remember that what is meant for you will not pass you by. That there is no "too late" in Divine timing.

Each day, you'll practice slowing your breath, releasing urgency, and listening for the rhythm beneath the rush.

May this week remind you that your timing is holy, and your path unfolds exactly as it should.

Day 1 – The False Clock

The Old Pattern

You've felt the ticking clock. The urgency. The comparison. The pressure to hurry up and get there already. You've judged your progress against someone else's timeline.

Who taught you that you are late?

The Sacred Shift

There is no "too late" in sacred time. The Divine doesn't rush, and your soul doesn't bloom on demand. The clock that tells you you're behind is not holy — it's a lie whispered by fear.

The Ritual Replacement

Journal Prompt: Where am I rushing? Who or what makes me feel like I'm behind?

Breathwork: Inhale slowly for 4 counts, hold for 4, exhale for 6. Repeat 5x, saying: "I return to the right timing."

Affirm: "I reject the false clock. I honor the rhythm of my soul."

Day 2 – The Seed Knows
When to Sprout

The Old Pattern

You've tried to force your growth. You've planted seeds and dug them up too soon, wondering why they haven't bloomed. Impatience made you doubt your process.

This is just a reminder: every seed sprouts in its own season. The oak does not rise at the same time a cucumber does.

The Sacred Shift

No seed is lazy. No sprout is late. The Earth does not rush what's becoming. You are a sacred seed, and your unfolding is wise beyond your conscious knowing.

The Ritual Replacement

Journal Prompt: What part of me feels like it should be "further along"? What if that belief is untrue?

Nature practice: Observe something growing. Witness its pace.

Affirm: "The seed knows. I trust my becoming."

Day 3 – The Pause Has Purpose

The Old Pattern

You've hated the waiting. The in-between. The liminal space where nothing seems to be happening. You've called it stuck, stagnant, or even failure.

The pause has purpose; it is the space to breathe so your story can continue.

The Sacred Shift

The pause is not punishment — it's preparation. In sacred timing, stillness holds power. The quiet between chapters is where Spirit rewrites your inner story.

The Ritual Replacement

Journal Prompt: When have I grown in ways I couldn't see until later?

Presence practice: Sit still for 5 minutes. Feel your breath. Say: "I honor the sacred pause."

Affirm: "Even when nothing is moving, something holy is unfolding in me."

Day 4 – Divine Detours Are
Still Sacred Paths

The Old Pattern

You've been frustrated by the setbacks. The reschedules, rejections, and reroutes. You've asked, "Why is this taking so long?" and "What am I doing wrong?"

Perhaps in those moments the of Divine detour, the truest question is not why, but what am I being invited to learn here?

The Sacred Shift

Delay is not denial. Detours are not failures. Sometimes, they are sacred protection. Sometimes, they are Spirit's way of aligning you with something better.

The Ritual Replacement

Journal Prompt: Where has life rerouted me — and what did I gain?

Object practice: Hold a stone or shell and whisper: "I bless the road I didn't expect."

Affirm: "I trust the detour. My soul knows the way."

Day 5 – Sacred Timing Includes You

The Old Pattern

You've believed the right moment will come only when you've done enough, healed enough, perfected enough.

You've delayed joy, waiting for "someday."

The Sacred Shift

Sacred Timing is not something outside of you — it includes you. It flows through you. The moment becomes right because you showed up.

The Ritual Replacement

Journal Prompt: Where am I waiting to be "ready"?

Embodiment: Stand grounded and say: "This moment is holy because I'm here."

Affirm: "I belong to this moment. I am not behind."

Day 6 – When You Stop Rushing, You Receive More

The Old Pattern

In your urgency, you've missed beauty. You've skipped over the miracle to get to the next milestone.

You've chased what might have unfolded if you had stayed still.

The Sacred Shift

Spirit isn't trying to withhold from you. It's trying to give to the real you — the one who can receive, not just achieve.

The Ritual Replacement

Journal Prompt: What in my life feels rushed or frantic?

Tea ritual: Consume something slowly, with gratitude.

Affirm: "When I stop rushing, I make room for grace."

Day 7 – The Time Is Now

The Old Pattern

You've waited for permission. For the stars to align.
For everything to be perfect before you let yourself begin.

Allow yourself to start even in the messiness.

The Sacred Shift

This moment is not lacking. Sacred timing is a rhythm that lives
inside your willingness to trust.

The Ritual Replacement

Journal Prompt: What wants to begin in me?

Action: Take one sacred step—no matter how small.

Affirm: "The time is now, and I am ready."

MY NOTES

WEEK 12: SELF-SABOTAGE →
DEVOTED ALIGNMENT

*"The real difficulty is to overcome how you think
about yourself." - Maya Angelou*

Self-sabotage often looks like laziness, fear, or failure — but
beneath it lies a wound. It is the part of you that tries to keep
you safe by pulling back just before the risk of joy, success, or
vulnerability. It was never meant to hurt you — only to
protect you.

This week, you are invited to meet self-sabotage with
compassion. You don't need harsher discipline; you need deeper
devotion. Alignment is not a forced march, it is a
sacred remembering of what your soul is here to embody.

Each day, you'll practice walking in agreement with your truth,
gently forgiving the parts of you that once thought safety meant
retreat.

May this week guide you from punishment into devotion, from
sabotage into sacred alignment.

Day 1 – The Pattern That Protects (and Punishes)

The Old Pattern

You've made progress, only to undo it. Set a goal, then ghost it. You've blamed laziness, fear, or lack of discipline. But beneath it all — there's a wounded part of you trying to stay safe.

Self-sabotage was never meant to hurt you. It was designed to protect you from visibility, disappointment, rejection, or even joy that felt too big.

The Sacred Shift

You don't need harsher discipline. You need deeper devotion. True alignment is not a forced march—it's a sacred remembering of what your soul is here to embody. You're not here to punish your way to progress. You're here to walk in sacred agreement with your truth.

The Ritual Replacement

Journal Prompt: Where have I sabotaged progress in the past? What was I trying to avoid or protect?

Body check-in: Gently place your hand over your heart and say: "I forgive the part of me that learned survival this way."

Affirm: "I choose devotion over discipline. My soul is safe in sacred alignment."

Day 2 – The Cost of the Almost

The Old Pattern

You have gotten close—almost launched the dream, told the truth, almost let yourself rise. But then came the backpedal. The delay. The "maybe later."

You have lived so many almosts that you've started believing they are safer than the real thing.

The Sacred Shift

The 'almost' is not your home. You were made to arrive. Spirit doesn't dangle your desires to torment you — it calls them forth to awaken you. Alignment isn't about being perfect. It's about saying yes, even when it's trembling. Even when it's incomplete.

The Ritual Replacement

Journal Prompt: Where in my life am I living in the "almost"? What do I believe will happen if I truly commit?

Mirror practice: Look at yourself and say, "I am no longer an almost. I arrive."

Affirm: "I step out of hesitation. I walk in holy yes."

Day 3 – The Fear of Being Too Much

The Old Pattern

You have dimmed your light before it could dazzle. You have diluted your truth so it would not disrupt. Deep down, you've worried that if you let the fullness of your gifts out, you'd be too much—or worse, abandoned.

Self-sabotage not just to stay small, but to stay safe. You however were always enough.

The Sacred Shift

You were never meant to be digestible to everyone. Your light isn't reckless — it's revelatory. The parts of you that feel "too much" are the very parts that carry your sacred medicine. You don't need to shrink. You need to devote yourself to the truth of your soul.

The Ritual Replacement

Journal Prompt: What parts of me have I hidden or softened for the comfort of others? What would it feel like to fully trust my bigness?

Voice activation: Speak your truth aloud — uncensored, even if messy. Whisper or shout. Let it move.

Affirm: "I am not too much. I am perfectly timed, divinely designed, and deeply worthy."

Day 4 – Patterns Are Not Prophecies

The Old Pattern

You've told yourself, "I always mess it up." You've replayed your past like it's a contract you're doomed to repeat. One mistake becomes an identity. One fall becomes a future forecast.

If you expect sabotage, it will alwawys shows up, dressed in your doubts.

The Sacred Shift

Your past may explain you, but it does not define you. Patterns are not prophecies. They are invitations. Each moment is a portal. You are not bound to repeat — you are invited to rechoose. Alignment happens in the now, not the never.

The Ritual Replacement

Journal Prompt: What "always" or "never" beliefs do I hold about myself? Where did they come from — and are they still true?

Release ritual: Write a self-limiting pattern on a small piece of paper and burn it (safely), saying: "This is not my future."

Affirm: "I rewrite my pattern through presence. I am free to become."

Day 5 – Sabotage Disguised
as Sacrifice

The Old Pattern

You've told yourself it's noble to give up your dreams for others.
To stay small so someone else can feel big.
To over-serve while under-nourishing your soul.

You've confused sabotage with sacrifice — and called it love.

The Sacred Shift

Sacrifice without alignment is self-abandonment. Love never asks you to disappear. Your sacred path will not require you to deny your truth. Real devotion includes you. It honors your wholeness, not your martyrdom.

The Ritual Replacement

Journal Prompt: Where have I sabotaged my growth in the name of loyalty or love?

Energy check-in: Place your hand over your solar plexus and ask, "Does this serve both them and me?"

Affirm: "I release false sacrifice. I honor my soul as sacred."

Day 6 – The Devotion Is the Discipline

The Old Pattern

You've waited to feel "motivated." You've told yourself you're lazy, inconsistent, or broken. You've treated your spiritual or creative work like something you must force, or else abandon when inspiration fades.

The truth is your devotion desearves a voice too.

The Sacred Shift

What if devotion is the discipline? Not harsh, rigid structure—but loving, steady return. You don't need to feel ready. You just need to return. Again and again, without shame. Your sacred path welcomes every step you're willing to take.

The Ritual Replacement

Journal Prompt: What do I long to return to? What would sacred consistency look like—not as punishment, but as love?

Action: Choose one devotion today — a 5-minute act of alignment.

Affirm: "I return without shame. My devotion is enough."

Day 7 – I Am Ready to Stop Fighting Myself

The Old Pattern

You've been at war within. One part of you pulls forward. The other resists, afraid. You've judged the fear, resented the resistance, and pushed harder, just to loop back again.

What if your self sabotage was never against you, but a misunderstood attempt at protection?

The Sacred Shift

Self-sabotage dissolves when self-trust grows. You don't have to fight your way into alignment. You can listen. Love. Integrate. There is nothing in you that needs to be conquered — only returned to wholeness.

The Ritual Replacement

Journal Prompt: What part of me feels afraid of rising? What might it need to feel safe?

Embody: Hug yourself. Literally. Whisper: "We're on the same team now."

Affirm: "I no longer fight myself. I rise as one."

MY NOTES

WEEK 13: RESISTANCE →
REBIRTH + INTEGRATION

"It's never too late to become who you want to be. You have the strength within to start over." -- F Scott Fitzgerald

At the edge of every transformation, resistance rises. It whispers that you've done enough, that it's too hard, that nothing will change. But resistance is not the end — it is the tremor before rebirth.

This week, you are invited to meet resistance not with shame, but with courage. To see it as proof that you are close, not far. Every wall you feel is built from old stories ready to fall away.

Each day, you'll step through the final threshold of this journey — not by force, but by faith.

May this week be your door of becoming, where resistance gives way to rebirth, and you rise into the fullness that was always yours.

Day 1 – The Final Wall

The Old Pattern

You've done the work. You've shown up. And yet... something
still resists. A voice whispers: "What if none of this changes
anything?" You feel the tug of retreat, the pull of patterns past.

This is the final wall — the one built from every story you've
outgrown.

The Sacred Shift

This isn't failure. This is friction at the edge of your becoming.
Resistance doesn't mean stop — it means you're close. The soul
trembles before it expands. Don't turn back now. This isn't just
the end of a cycle — it's the door to your rebirth.

The Ritual Replacement

Journal Prompt: What resistance am I feeling right now? What
part of me is afraid to complete this transformation?
Light a candle and say, "I honor the threshold. I am ready to pass
through," or "I do not fear my fullness. I rise beyond resistance."

Day 2 – When Growth Looks Like Loss

The Old Pattern

There's a hidden belief that growth should feel good. That transformation should look clean, beautiful, even celebrated. But sometimes, what grows must first fall away. You may feel grief, confusion, or quiet sadness.

You are allowed to offer compassion to the self who carried you through survival and bless them for all they endured.

The Sacred Shift

Loss doesn't mean you're off track—it means you're making space. What leaves may not be failure. It may be the shell you outgrew. The soul doesn't cling to what no longer fits. It surrenders. And in the surrender, it finds wings.

The Ritual Replacement

Journal Prompt: What have I recently released or lost? What am I learning from its absence?

Simple ritual: Place your hands over your heart and say, "I bless what has gone. I trust what is to come."

Affirm: "Even in loss, I am being led. Even in letting go, I am becoming."

Day 3 – The Part of Me That Survived

The Old Pattern

You've tried to evolve without looking back. To step into the sacred and leave behind the shadow—but part of you still clings to the old ways. The survivor. The fighter. The one who got you through when there was no light.

You wonder: Do I have to let them go to rise?

The Sacred Shift

You do not need to kill the survivor to become the creator. They are not your enemy — they're your root. Integration means you carry the wisdom, but not the fear. You invite them into peace. They don't need to run anymore. They can rest. You can rise.

The Ritual Replacement

Journal Prompt: What part of me kept me safe — but is no longer needed in the same way? What do they need to hear now?

Mirror practice: Look into your eyes and say, "Thank you for surviving. You may rest now. We rise together."

Affirm: "I honor the one who endured. I become the one who creates."

Day 4 – Rebirth Isn't a Bang. It is a Breath.

The Old Pattern

You have been waiting for fireworks. A moment where everything shifts, loudly and finally. You have thought, "When it happens, I'll know."

Rebirth rarely looks like an explosion. It looks like exhaling. Like finally unclenching. Like peace arriving where panic used to live.

The Sacred Shift

Rebirth doesn't always announce itself. Sometimes, it whispers. It comes in quiet choices, in steady healing, in the stillness after the storm. Trust the soft returns. The sacred is often subtle.

The Ritual Replacement

Journal Prompt: What gentle signs of rebirth have I experienced lately? Where am I now new, even if it is quiet?

Breath ritual: Inhale deeply, hold, then exhale with sound. Say, "I choose the path of peace."

Affirm: "My rebirth is not loud — but it is real."

Day 5 – I Am Becoming the Voice

The Old Pattern

You have long hidden the truth of who you are. Out of fear. Out of protection. Out of the belief that your voice was too much — or not enough. But the time of muting is over.

The story must be told. The only one who can tell it is you.

The Sacred Shift

Your voice is not just sound, it is soul. When you speak truth, you reclaim lifetimes. When you write, weep, or roar with clarity, you don't just free yourself — you open the way for others. This is more than expression. This is remembrance.

The Ritual Replacement

Journal Prompt: What have I been afraid to say or share? What part of my truth is rising now?

Expression: Sing, speak, or write one thing aloud today that you once silenced.

Affirm: "I am the voice I once needed. I speak with soul and sovereignty."

Day 6 – Integration Is a Spiral

The Old Pattern

You want to be done. To be healed. To be finished. But then something old returns — a feeling, a fear — and you wonder: "Haven't I already dealt with this?" You mistake the spiral for a setback.

Every plant undergoes pruning, not as a punishment from the gardner, but as mercy that makes room for new growth.

The Sacred Shift

Integration is not a straight line. It's a spiral. You revisit, not because you failed, but because you're ready to go deeper. Each return brings new light. This is not the same version of you — it's the wiser one.

The Ritual Replacement

Journal Prompt: What patterns or emotions have resurfaced lately? How am I relating to them differently now?

Action: Draw a spiral on paper and write inside it: "I trust the return."

Affirm: "I walk the spiral path with grace. I grow deeper each time."

Day 7 – I Am the Integration

The Old Pattern

You thought the end would feel final. Like the closing of a door. But it feels more like breath. Like standing in your skin without needing to explain. Like knowing, "This is who I am now."

Remember, the soul does not arrive -- it unfolds. Each step is a nearness, not an ending.

The Sacred Shift

There is no final chapter — only a deeper presence. You are not leaving the work behind. You are the work. You are the sacred pattern rewritten. The shadow transmuted. The prayer that kept going.

The Ritual Replacement

Journal Prompt: What has this journey shown me about who I truly am? How will I honor this becoming?

Blessing: Write your own closing words. Let it be a vow.
A return. A beginning.

Affirm: "I am the integration. I carry the sacred within me."

MY NOTES

THE SPACE BETWEEN WORLDS

You have walked through the fire of old patterns.
You've named them. Held them. Released them.

And now...

You stand between what was and what might become.
In this sacred pause — this liminal breath — you are not lost.
You are being rewoven. Spirit speaks now not through
thunder, but through stillness.

And it says:

You are not broken — you are becoming.
You are not too late — you are right on time.
You are not alone — I have sent others to walk with you.
This is not the end. This is the turning of the page.

Journal Prompt:

What part of me is rising from the ashes of who I used to be?
What truth do I hear in the silence?

Write without rushing. Let your soul answer.

REFLECTION – RETURNING
TO THE ROOM

There's a moment when the sacred meets the strange…

When you return to the place of your pain
—and the air feels different.

You sit in the same chair. You look out the same window.
But the echo is softer now. The space
doesn't bite the way it used to.

That's not just healing. That's transformation.

You are no longer who you were. You're the version of
you who can sit in the old room — and not disappear.

You are not haunted here. You are holy here.

TO THE SOUL THAT CHOSE
TO REMEMBER

You have walked these ninety days, through
shadowed doubt and sacred blaze —

Know this:

You are not broken. You are blooming.
The wounds that once silenced you
Have become songs of survival.
The habits that held you small
Now kneel at the feet of your holy expansion.
You did not come here to escape the dark.
You came to light a candle inside it.

And now,
With breath steady and spirit clear,
You carry the sacred not just in your habits —
But in your ordinary moments,
Your choices, your voice, your becoming.

So let this be your vow:

I will no longer hide from my wholeness.
I will honor what I've released and cherish what remains.
I will live as one who remembers the sacred
in all things, even myself.

And so it is.

AFTERWORD

As I close these pages, I want to thank you for walking this path with me. To name the shadow and reclaim the sacred is no small thing, it is an act of courage, of honesty, of becoming.

But this is not the end. This is a beginning.

With the shadows tended and the sacred unveiled, new ground has been cleared. In the next volume, Sacred Repatterning, we will step into the art of weaving new habits for your soul, aligning with the elements, the rhythms of the stars, to dream, and rebuild what has been waiting to rise within you.

I invite you to join me there, carrying the wisdom of your shadows and the light of your sacred becoming into the next chapter of your journey.

ACKNOWLEDGEMENT

To the shadows that shaped me —
Thank you for revealing what was hidden
and leading me home to my light.

To the voices who said I was too much, not enough, or
unworthy —
You became the fire and anvil where I
remembered who I truly am.

To those I love deeply, whose presence was the compass through
every darkened chapter —
Thank you for your love, your grace.

To you who have started your journey, and every
sacred soul who chooses to rise with intention—this is for you.

To the weary soul, may these pages be water.

To the searching heart, these words may be light.

To the hidden self, may you find this space to be safe.

You are not broken.

You are becoming.